"To walk in nature is to witness a thousand miracles."

MARY DAVIS

HOW TO USE THIS BOOK

This log book has been created for you to keep a personal journal of your amazing hiking adventures. Share it with friends, keep it for memories, or use it as a reference book of all the trails you have walked.

It's split into four sections for easy use.

First up you'll see the Hiking Log Index. This is where you simply record the date and name of your hike for quick reference. You can also favorite a route with a ⭐ to remind yourself which trails you particularly enjoyed.

Then there's the Hiking Logs section which contains 52 individually numbered records. Each log has space for documenting your hike, including trail details, weather conditions, who you were with and facilities along the way. You can then give your hike an overall rating. There's also plenty of space for you to log your own experiences and observations, along with a photo or drawing.

Towards the back of the book is a Hiking Tips reference section with advice about safety, essential gear, and how best to walk a trail. Next there's Hiking Lingo that has a list of common terms, so if you don't know what 'camel up', 'hiker legs', or 'sand-bagging' mean, this is the section for you. The final page is for you to create your very own Hiking Bucket List of the trails you'd love to hike in the future.

The best place for you to start your hiking log book is by filling out the details below.

Happy hiking!

THIS BOOK BELONGS TO:

____

IF FOUND PLEASE CONTACT ME BY:

____

HIKING LOG INDEX

LOG #	DATE:	HIKE/TRAIL NAME:	
1			☆
2			☆
3			☆
4			☆
5			☆
6			☆
7			☆
8			☆
9			☆
10			☆
11			☆
12			☆
13			☆
14			☆
15			☆
16			☆
17			☆
18			☆
19			☆
20			☆
21			☆
22			☆
23			☆
24			☆
25			☆
26			☆

LOG #	DATE:	HIKE/TRAIL NAME:	
27			☆
28			☆
29			☆
30			☆
31			☆
32			☆
33			☆
34			☆
35			☆
36			☆
37			☆
38			☆
39			☆
40			☆
41			☆
42			☆
43			☆
44			☆
45			☆
46			☆
47			☆
48			☆
49			☆
50			☆
51			☆
52			☆

HIKING LOG #1

HIKE/TRAIL NAME: ____

DATE: ________________   TYPE: ONE WAY   LOOP   OUT & BACK   OVERNIGHT

START TIME: __________   LOCATION: ___________________________
(OR GPS)

END TIME: __________   LOCATION: ___________________________
(OR GPS)

DISTANCE: __________   ELEVATION: __________ ⇑   __________ ⇓

WEATHER:

TRAIL CONDITION: WILD   ◯ ◯ ◯ ◯ ◯   WELL USED

TRAIL TRAFFIC: LIGHT   ◯ ◯ ◯ ◯ ◯   HEAVY

DIFFICULTY LEVEL: EASY   ◯ ◯ ◯ ◯ ◯   HARD

FUN FACTOR: DULL   ◯ ◯ ◯ ◯ ◯   AMAZING

TRAIL RESERVATION REQUIRED?   YES / NO

CAMPING PERMIT REQUIRED?   YES / NO

CELL RECEPTION: HIKING BUDDIES:
____
FACILITIES:
____

____

____

____

OVERALL RATING:

PHOTO / DRAWING:

NOTES & OBSERVATIONS:

MEMORABLE MOMENT:

HIKING LOG #2

HIKE/TRAIL NAME: ______________________________

DATE: ________________ TYPE: → ↻ ⇄ ⛺
ONE WAY   LOOP   OUT & BACK   OVERNIGHT

START TIME: __________ LOCATION: ________________
(OR GPS)

END TIME: __________ LOCATION: ________________
(OR GPS)

DISTANCE: __________ ELEVATION: __________ ⇧ __________ ⇩

WEATHER:

TRAIL CONDITION: WILD ○ ○ ○ ○ ○ WELL USED

TRAIL TRAFFIC: LIGHT ○ ○ ○ ○ ○ HEAVY

DIFFICULTY LEVEL: EASY ○ ○ ○ ○ ○ HARD

FUN FACTOR: DULL ○ ○ ○ ○ ○ AMAZING

TRAIL RESERVATION REQUIRED? YES / NO

CAMPING PERMIT REQUIRED? YES / NO

CELL RECEPTION: HIKING BUDDIES:

____

____

FACILITIES: ______________________________

____

____

OVERALL RATING:

PHOTO / DRAWING:

NOTES & OBSERVATIONS:

MEMORABLE MOMENT:

HIKING LOG #3

HIKE/TRAIL NAME: _______________________________

DATE: _______________ TYPE: ONE WAY   LOOP   OUT & BACK   OVERNIGHT

START TIME: _____________ LOCATION: _______________________
(OR GPS)

END TIME: _____________ LOCATION: _______________________
(OR GPS)

DISTANCE: _____________ ELEVATION: _________ ⇧ _________ ⇩

WEATHER:

TRAIL CONDITION: WILD ○ ○ ○ ○ ○ WELL USED

TRAIL TRAFFIC: LIGHT ○ ○ ○ ○ ○ HEAVY

DIFFICULTY LEVEL: EASY ○ ○ ○ ○ ○ HARD

FUN FACTOR: DULL ○ ○ ○ ○ ○ AMAZING

TRAIL RESERVATION REQUIRED? YES / NO

CAMPING PERMIT REQUIRED? YES / NO

CELL RECEPTION: HIKING BUDDIES:

FACILITIES:

____

____

____

____

____

OVERALL RATING:

NOTES & OBSERVATIONS:

MEMORABLE MOMENT:

HIKING LOG #4

HIKE/TRAIL NAME: _______________________

DATE: _______________ TYPE: ONE WAY   LOOP   OUT & BACK   OVERNIGHT

START TIME: __________ LOCATION: _______________
(OR GPS)

END TIME: __________ LOCATION: _______________
(OR GPS)

DISTANCE: __________ ELEVATION: ________ ⇧ ________ ⇩

WEATHER:

TRAIL CONDITION: WILD ◯ ◯ ◯ ◯ ◯ WELL USED

TRAIL TRAFFIC: LIGHT ◯ ◯ ◯ ◯ ◯ HEAVY

DIFFICULTY LEVEL: EASY ◯ ◯ ◯ ◯ ◯ HARD

FUN FACTOR: DULL ◯ ◯ ◯ ◯ ◯ AMAZING

TRAIL RESERVATION REQUIRED?   YES / NO

CAMPING PERMIT REQUIRED?   YES / NO

CELL RECEPTION: HIKING BUDDIES:
____
____
FACILITIES:
____
____
____
____

OVERALL RATING:

PHOTO / DRAWING:

NOTES & OBSERVATIONS:

MEMORABLE MOMENT:

HIKING LOG #5

HIKE/TRAIL NAME: _______________________________

DATE: _______________   TYPE: → ONE WAY   ↻ LOOP   ⇄ OUT & BACK   OVERNIGHT

START TIME: _______________   LOCATION: _______________
(OR GPS)

END TIME: _______________   LOCATION: _______________
(OR GPS)

DISTANCE: _______________   ELEVATION: _______________ ⇧ _______________ ⇩

WEATHER:

TRAIL CONDITION: WILD   ○ ○ ○ ○ ○   WELL USED

TRAIL TRAFFIC: LIGHT   ○ ○ ○ ○ ○   HEAVY

DIFFICULTY LEVEL: EASY   ○ ○ ○ ○ ○   HARD

FUN FACTOR: DULL   ○ ○ ○ ○ ○   AMAZING

TRAIL RESERVATION REQUIRED?   YES / NO

CAMPING PERMIT REQUIRED?   YES / NO

CELL RECEPTION: HIKING BUDDIES:

FACILITIES:

____

____

____

____

____

OVERALL RATING:

PHOTO / DRAWING:

NOTES & OBSERVATIONS:

MEMORABLE MOMENT:

HIKING LOG #6

HIKE/TRAIL NAME: _______________________________

DATE: _______________

TYPE: → ONE WAY   ↻ LOOP   ⇄ OUT & BACK   OVERNIGHT

START TIME: _______________   LOCATION: _______________
(OR GPS)

END TIME: _______________   LOCATION: _______________
(OR GPS)

DISTANCE: _______________   ELEVATION: _______ ⇧ _______ ⇩

WEATHER:

TRAIL CONDITION: WILD   ○ ○ ○ ○ ○   WELL USED

TRAIL TRAFFIC: LIGHT   ○ ○ ○ ○ ○   HEAVY

DIFFICULTY LEVEL: EASY   ○ ○ ○ ○ ○   HARD

FUN FACTOR: DULL   ○ ○ ○ ○ ○   AMAZING

TRAIL RESERVATION REQUIRED?   YES / NO

CAMPING PERMIT REQUIRED?   YES / NO

CELL RECEPTION: HIKING BUDDIES:

FACILITIES:

____

____

____

____

____

OVERALL RATING:

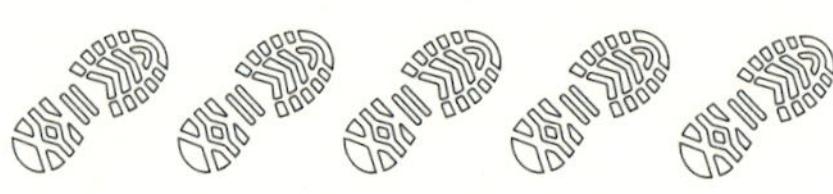

PHOTO / DRAWING:

NOTES & OBSERVATIONS:

MEMORABLE MOMENT:

HIKING LOG #7

HIKE/TRAIL NAME: _______________________________

DATE: _______________ TYPE: ONE WAY   LOOP   OUT & BACK   OVERNIGHT

START TIME: __________ LOCATION: _______________________
(OR GPS)

END TIME: __________ LOCATION: _______________________
(OR GPS)

DISTANCE: __________ ELEVATION: _________ ⇧ _________ ⇩

WEATHER:

TRAIL CONDITION: WILD ○ ○ ○ ○ ○ WELL USED

TRAIL TRAFFIC: LIGHT ○ ○ ○ ○ ○ HEAVY

DIFFICULTY LEVEL: EASY ○ ○ ○ ○ ○ HARD

FUN FACTOR: DULL ○ ○ ○ ○ ○ AMAZING

TRAIL RESERVATION REQUIRED?   YES / NO

CAMPING PERMIT REQUIRED?   YES / NO

CELL RECEPTION: HIKING BUDDIES:

____

____

FACILITIES:

____

____

____

____

OVERALL RATING:

PHOTO / DRAWING:

NOTES & OBSERVATIONS:

MEMORABLE MOMENT:

HIKING LOG #8

HIKE/TRAIL NAME: _______________________________

DATE: _______________ TYPE: → ONE WAY   ↻ LOOP   ⇄ OUT & BACK   OVERNIGHT

START TIME: _______________ LOCATION: _______________
(OR GPS)

END TIME: _______________ LOCATION: _______________
(OR GPS)

DISTANCE: _______________ ELEVATION: _______ ⇧ _______ ⇩

WEATHER: ☀ ⛅ ☁ 🌧 ⛈ ❄ 🌡_______

TRAIL CONDITION: WILD ○ ○ ○ ○ ○ WELL USED

TRAIL TRAFFIC: LIGHT ○ ○ ○ ○ ○ HEAVY

DIFFICULTY LEVEL: EASY ○ ○ ○ ○ ○ HARD

FUN FACTOR: DULL ○ ○ ○ ○ ○ AMAZING

TRAIL RESERVATION REQUIRED? YES / NO

CAMPING PERMIT REQUIRED? YES / NO

CELL RECEPTION: 📶 HIKING BUDDIES:

FACILITIES: _______________________________

____

____

____

OVERALL RATING: 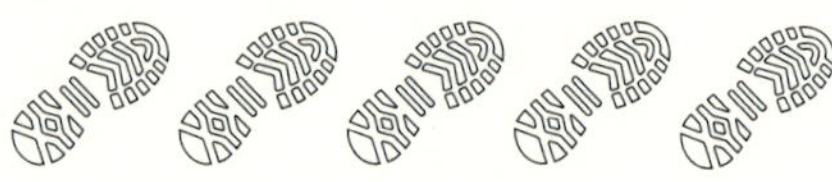

PHOTO / DRAWING:

NOTES & OBSERVATIONS:

MEMORABLE MOMENT:

HIKING LOG #9

HIKE/TRAIL NAME: _______________________________________

DATE: ___________________   TYPE: → ONE WAY   ↻ LOOP   ⇄ OUT & BACK   ⛺ OVERNIGHT

START TIME: ____________   LOCATION: _______________________
                             (OR GPS)

END TIME: ____________   LOCATION: _______________________
                           (OR GPS)

DISTANCE: ____________   ELEVATION: __________ ⇧ __________ ⇩

WEATHER: ☀   ⛅   ☁   🌧   ⛈   ❄   🌡 ________

TRAIL CONDITION:	WILD	○ ○ ○ ○ ○	WELL USED
TRAIL TRAFFIC:	LIGHT	○ ○ ○ ○ ○	HEAVY
DIFFICULTY LEVEL:	EASY	○ ○ ○ ○ ○	HARD
FUN FACTOR:	DULL	○ ○ ○ ○ ○	AMAZING

TRAIL RESERVATION REQUIRED?   YES / NO

CAMPING PERMIT REQUIRED?   YES / NO

CELL RECEPTION: 📶   HIKING BUDDIES:

FACILITIES:
____
🅿 🚻 🐾
____
🚰 🏕 ⛺
____

____

____

OVERALL RATING: 

PHOTO / DRAWING:

NOTES & OBSERVATIONS:

MEMORABLE MOMENT:

HIKING LOG #10

HIKE/TRAIL NAME: _______________________

DATE: _______________ TYPE: → ONE WAY ↻ LOOP ⇄ OUT & BACK ⛺ OVERNIGHT

START TIME: ___________ LOCATION: _______________
(OR GPS)

END TIME: ___________ LOCATION: _______________
(OR GPS)

DISTANCE: ___________ ELEVATION: _________ ⇧ _________ ⇩

WEATHER: ☀ ⛅ ☁ 🌧 ⛈ ❄ 🌡 ___________

TRAIL CONDITION: WILD ◯ ◯ ◯ ◯ ◯ WELL USED

TRAIL TRAFFIC: LIGHT ◯ ◯ ◯ ◯ ◯ HEAVY

DIFFICULTY LEVEL: EASY ◯ ◯ ◯ ◯ ◯ HARD

FUN FACTOR: DULL ◯ ◯ ◯ ◯ ◯ AMAZING

TRAIL RESERVATION REQUIRED? YES / NO

CAMPING PERMIT REQUIRED? YES / NO

CELL RECEPTION: ▁▂▃▅ HIKING BUDDIES:
____
FACILITIES: _______________________
____
____
____
____

OVERALL RATING:
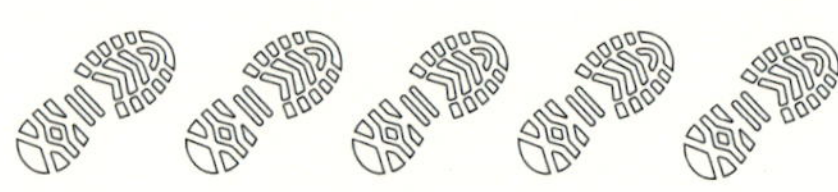

PHOTO / DRAWING:

NOTES & OBSERVATIONS:

MEMORABLE MOMENT:

HIKING LOG #11

HIKE/TRAIL NAME: _______________________________

DATE: _______________   TYPE: ONE WAY   LOOP   OUT & BACK   OVERNIGHT

START TIME: _______________   LOCATION: _______________
(OR GPS)

END TIME: _______________   LOCATION: _______________
(OR GPS)

DISTANCE: _______________   ELEVATION: _______________ ⇧   _______________ ⇩

WEATHER:

TRAIL CONDITION: WILD ○ ○ ○ ○ ○ WELL USED

TRAIL TRAFFIC: LIGHT ○ ○ ○ ○ ○ HEAVY

DIFFICULTY LEVEL: EASY ○ ○ ○ ○ ○ HARD

FUN FACTOR: DULL ○ ○ ○ ○ ○ AMAZING

TRAIL RESERVATION REQUIRED?   YES / NO

CAMPING PERMIT REQUIRED?   YES / NO

CELL RECEPTION: HIKING BUDDIES:

FACILITIES:
____
____
____
____

OVERALL RATING: 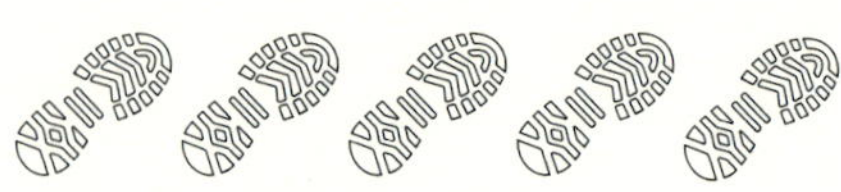

PHOTO / DRAWING:

NOTES & OBSERVATIONS:

MEMORABLE MOMENT:

HIKING LOG #12

HIKE/TRAIL NAME: _______________________

DATE: _______________ TYPE: ONE WAY   LOOP   OUT & BACK   OVERNIGHT

START TIME: _______________ LOCATION: _______________
(OR GPS)

END TIME: _______________ LOCATION: _______________
(OR GPS)

DISTANCE: _______________ ELEVATION: _______ ⇧ _______ ⇩

WEATHER:

TRAIL CONDITION: WILD ○ ○ ○ ○ ○ WELL USED

TRAIL TRAFFIC: LIGHT ○ ○ ○ ○ ○ HEAVY

DIFFICULTY LEVEL: EASY ○ ○ ○ ○ ○ HARD

FUN FACTOR: DULL ○ ○ ○ ○ ○ AMAZING

TRAIL RESERVATION REQUIRED? YES / NO

CAMPING PERMIT REQUIRED? YES / NO

CELL RECEPTION: HIKING BUDDIES:

____

____

FACILITIES: _______________________

____

____

____

OVERALL RATING:

PHOTO / DRAWING:

NOTES & OBSERVATIONS:

MEMORABLE MOMENT:

HIKING LOG #13

HIKE/TRAIL NAME: _______________________________________

DATE: ___________________   TYPE: → ONE WAY   ↻ LOOP   ⇄ OUT & BACK   ⛺ OVERNIGHT

START TIME: ___________   LOCATION: _______________________
(OR GPS)

END TIME: ___________   LOCATION: _______________________
(OR GPS)

DISTANCE: ___________   ELEVATION: ___________ ⇧ ___________ ⇩

WEATHER: ☀   ⛅   ☁   🌧   ⛈   ❄   🌡 ___________

TRAIL CONDITION: WILD   ○ ○ ○ ○ ○   WELL USED

TRAIL TRAFFIC: LIGHT   ○ ○ ○ ○ ○   HEAVY

DIFFICULTY LEVEL: EASY   ○ ○ ○ ○ ○   HARD

FUN FACTOR: DULL   ○ ○ ○ ○ ○   AMAZING

TRAIL RESERVATION REQUIRED?   YES / NO

CAMPING PERMIT REQUIRED?   YES / NO

CELL RECEPTION: HIKING BUDDIES:
____

FACILITIES: _______________________

____

____

____

____

OVERALL RATING:

PHOTO / DRAWING:

NOTES & OBSERVATIONS:

MEMORABLE MOMENT:

HIKING LOG #14

HIKE/TRAIL NAME: _______________________________

DATE: _______________ TYPE: ONE WAY   LOOP   OUT & BACK   OVERNIGHT

START TIME: _________ LOCATION: _______________
(OR GPS)

END TIME: _________ LOCATION: _______________
(OR GPS)

DISTANCE: _________ ELEVATION: _______ ⇧ _______ ⇩

WEATHER:

TRAIL CONDITION: WILD ○ ○ ○ ○ ○ WELL USED

TRAIL TRAFFIC: LIGHT ○ ○ ○ ○ ○ HEAVY

DIFFICULTY LEVEL: EASY ○ ○ ○ ○ ○ HARD

FUN FACTOR: DULL ○ ○ ○ ○ ○ AMAZING

TRAIL RESERVATION REQUIRED? YES / NO

CAMPING PERMIT REQUIRED? YES / NO

CELL RECEPTION: HIKING BUDDIES:

FACILITIES:
____
____
____
____
____

OVERALL RATING:

PHOTO / DRAWING:

NOTES & OBSERVATIONS:

MEMORABLE MOMENT:

HIKING LOG #15

HIKE/TRAIL NAME: _______________________________

DATE: _______________ TYPE: → ONE WAY   ↻ LOOP   ⇄ OUT & BACK   ⛺ OVERNIGHT

START TIME: ___________ LOCATION: _______________________
(OR GPS)

END TIME: ___________ LOCATION: _______________________
(OR GPS)

DISTANCE: ___________ ELEVATION: __________ ⇧ __________ ⇩

WEATHER:

TRAIL CONDITION: WILD ◯ ◯ ◯ ◯ ◯ WELL USED

TRAIL TRAFFIC: LIGHT ◯ ◯ ◯ ◯ ◯ HEAVY

DIFFICULTY LEVEL: EASY ◯ ◯ ◯ ◯ ◯ HARD

FUN FACTOR: DULL ◯ ◯ ◯ ◯ ◯ AMAZING

TRAIL RESERVATION REQUIRED?   YES / NO

CAMPING PERMIT REQUIRED?   YES / NO

CELL RECEPTION: HIKING BUDDIES:

FACILITIES:

____

____

____

____

____

____

OVERALL RATING:

PHOTO / DRAWING:

NOTES & OBSERVATIONS:

MEMORABLE MOMENT:

HIKING LOG #16

HIKE/TRAIL NAME: _______________________________

DATE: _______________ TYPE: ONE WAY LOOP OUT & BACK OVERNIGHT

START TIME: _______________ LOCATION: _______________
(OR GPS)

END TIME: _______________ LOCATION: _______________
(OR GPS)

DISTANCE: _______________ ELEVATION: _______________ ⇧ _______________ ⇩

WEATHER:

TRAIL CONDITION: WILD ◯ ◯ ◯ ◯ ◯   WELL USED

TRAIL TRAFFIC: LIGHT ◯ ◯ ◯ ◯ ◯   HEAVY

DIFFICULTY LEVEL: EASY ◯ ◯ ◯ ◯ ◯   HARD

FUN FACTOR: DULL ◯ ◯ ◯ ◯ ◯   AMAZING

TRAIL RESERVATION REQUIRED?   YES / NO

CAMPING PERMIT REQUIRED?   YES / NO

CELL RECEPTION: HIKING BUDDIES:
____

FACILITIES:
____

____

____

____

____

OVERALL RATING: 

PHOTO / DRAWING:

NOTES & OBSERVATIONS:

MEMORABLE MOMENT:

HIKING LOG #17

HIKE/TRAIL NAME: _______________________________

DATE: _______________ TYPE: ONE WAY   LOOP   OUT & BACK   OVERNIGHT

START TIME: _____________ LOCATION: _______________________
(OR GPS)

END TIME: _____________ LOCATION: _______________________
(OR GPS)

DISTANCE: _____________ ELEVATION: _______ ⇧ _______ ⇩

WEATHER:

TRAIL CONDITION: WILD ◯ ◯ ◯ ◯ ◯ WELL USED

TRAIL TRAFFIC: LIGHT ◯ ◯ ◯ ◯ ◯ HEAVY

DIFFICULTY LEVEL: EASY ◯ ◯ ◯ ◯ ◯ HARD

FUN FACTOR: DULL ◯ ◯ ◯ ◯ ◯ AMAZING

TRAIL RESERVATION REQUIRED? YES / NO

CAMPING PERMIT REQUIRED? YES / NO

CELL RECEPTION: HIKING BUDDIES:

FACILITIES:
____
____
____
____
____

OVERALL RATING: 

PHOTO / DRAWING:

NOTES & OBSERVATIONS:

MEMORABLE MOMENT:

HIKING LOG #18

HIKE/TRAIL NAME: _______________________

DATE: _______________ TYPE: ONE WAY   LOOP   OUT & BACK   OVERNIGHT

START TIME: __________ LOCATION: _______________
(OR GPS)

END TIME: __________ LOCATION: _______________
(OR GPS)

DISTANCE: __________ ELEVATION: __________ ⇧ __________ ⇩

WEATHER:

TRAIL CONDITION: WILD ○ ○ ○ ○ ○ WELL USED

TRAIL TRAFFIC: LIGHT ○ ○ ○ ○ ○ HEAVY

DIFFICULTY LEVEL: EASY ○ ○ ○ ○ ○ HARD

FUN FACTOR: DULL ○ ○ ○ ○ ○ AMAZING

TRAIL RESERVATION REQUIRED?   YES / NO

CAMPING PERMIT REQUIRED?   YES / NO

CELL RECEPTION: HIKING BUDDIES:

____

____

FACILITIES:

____

____

____

____

OVERALL RATING:

PHOTO / DRAWING:

NOTES & OBSERVATIONS:

MEMORABLE MOMENT:

HIKING LOG #19

HIKE/TRAIL NAME: ____

DATE: _________________ TYPE: → ONE WAY   ↻ LOOP   ⇄ OUT & BACK   OVERNIGHT

START TIME: __________ LOCATION: _______________________________
(OR GPS)

END TIME: __________ LOCATION: _________________________________
(OR GPS)

DISTANCE: __________ ELEVATION: __________ ⇧ __________ ⇩

WEATHER: ☀ ⛅ ☁ 🌧 ⛈ ❄ 🌡 __________

TRAIL CONDITION: WILD   ◯ ◯ ◯ ◯ ◯   WELL USED

TRAIL TRAFFIC: LIGHT   ◯ ◯ ◯ ◯ ◯   HEAVY

DIFFICULTY LEVEL: EASY   ◯ ◯ ◯ ◯ ◯   HARD

FUN FACTOR: DULL   ◯ ◯ ◯ ◯ ◯   AMAZING

TRAIL RESERVATION REQUIRED?   YES / NO

CAMPING PERMIT REQUIRED?   YES / NO

CELL RECEPTION:

FACILITIES:

HIKING BUDDIES: _________________________________
____
____
____
____
____

OVERALL RATING:

PHOTO / DRAWING:

NOTES & OBSERVATIONS:

MEMORABLE MOMENT:

HIKING LOG #20

HIKE/TRAIL NAME: ____

DATE: _______________   TYPE: → ONE WAY   ↻ LOOP   ⇄ OUT & BACK   OVERNIGHT

START TIME: _______________   LOCATION: _______________________________
(OR GPS)

END TIME: _______________   LOCATION: _______________________________
(OR GPS)

DISTANCE: _______________   ELEVATION: _______________ ⇧   _______________ ⇩

WEATHER:

TRAIL CONDITION: WILD   ◯ ◯ ◯ ◯ ◯   WELL USED

TRAIL TRAFFIC: LIGHT   ◯ ◯ ◯ ◯ ◯   HEAVY

DIFFICULTY LEVEL: EASY   ◯ ◯ ◯ ◯ ◯   HARD

FUN FACTOR: DULL   ◯ ◯ ◯ ◯ ◯   AMAZING

TRAIL RESERVATION REQUIRED?   YES / NO

CAMPING PERMIT REQUIRED?   YES / NO

CELL RECEPTION:

HIKING BUDDIES:

____
____
____
____
____
____

FACILITIES:

OVERALL RATING:

PHOTO / DRAWING:

NOTES & OBSERVATIONS:

MEMORABLE MOMENT:

HIKING LOG #21

HIKE/TRAIL NAME: _______________________________

DATE: _________________ TYPE: → ONE WAY   ↻ LOOP   ⇄ OUT & BACK   ⛺ OVERNIGHT

START TIME: _________ LOCATION: _______________________
(OR GPS)

END TIME: _________ LOCATION: _______________________
(OR GPS)

DISTANCE: _________ ELEVATION: _________ ⇧ _________ ⇩

WEATHER: ☀ ⛅ ☁ 🌧 ⛈ ❄ 🌡 _______

TRAIL CONDITION: WILD   ○ ○ ○ ○ ○   WELL USED

TRAIL TRAFFIC: LIGHT   ○ ○ ○ ○ ○   HEAVY

DIFFICULTY LEVEL: EASY   ○ ○ ○ ○ ○   HARD

FUN FACTOR: DULL   ○ ○ ○ ○ ○   AMAZING

TRAIL RESERVATION REQUIRED?   YES / NO

CAMPING PERMIT REQUIRED?   YES / NO

CELL RECEPTION: 📶   HIKING BUDDIES:
____
____
FACILITIES: _______________________
____
____
____

OVERALL RATING: 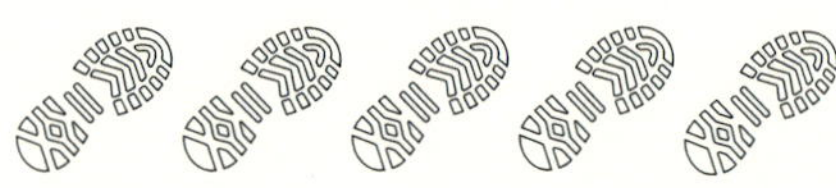

PHOTO / DRAWING:

NOTES & OBSERVATIONS:

MEMORABLE MOMENT:

HIKING LOG #22

HIKE/TRAIL NAME: ___________________________________

DATE: _______________   TYPE: → ONE WAY   ↻ LOOP   ⇄ OUT & BACK   ⛺ OVERNIGHT

START TIME: _______________   LOCATION: _______________
(OR GPS)

END TIME: _______________   LOCATION: _______________
(OR GPS)

DISTANCE: _______________   ELEVATION: _______________ ⇧ _______________ ⇩

WEATHER: ☀ ⛅ ☁ 🌧 ⛈ ❄ 🌡

TRAIL CONDITION: WILD   ○ ○ ○ ○ ○   WELL USED

TRAIL TRAFFIC: LIGHT   ○ ○ ○ ○ ○   HEAVY

DIFFICULTY LEVEL: EASY   ○ ○ ○ ○ ○   HARD

FUN FACTOR: DULL   ○ ○ ○ ○ ○   AMAZING

TRAIL RESERVATION REQUIRED?   YES / NO

CAMPING PERMIT REQUIRED?   YES / NO

CELL RECEPTION: 📶   HIKING BUDDIES:

FACILITIES:
____
____
____
____
____
____

OVERALL RATING:

PHOTO / DRAWING:

NOTES & OBSERVATIONS:

MEMORABLE MOMENT:

HIKING LOG #23

HIKE/TRAIL NAME: ___________________________

DATE: _______________ TYPE: → ONE WAY   ↻ LOOP   ⇄ OUT & BACK   ⛺ OVERNIGHT

START TIME: _________ LOCATION: ___________________
(OR GPS)

END TIME: _________ LOCATION: ___________________
(OR GPS)

DISTANCE: _________ ELEVATION: _________ ⇧ _________ ⇩

WEATHER: ☀ ⛅ ☁ 🌧 ⛈ ❄ 🌡 ___________

TRAIL CONDITION:	WILD	○	○	○	○	○	WELL USED
TRAIL TRAFFIC:	LIGHT	○	○	○	○	○	HEAVY
DIFFICULTY LEVEL:	EASY	○	○	○	○	○	HARD
FUN FACTOR:	DULL	○	○	○	○	○	AMAZING

TRAIL RESERVATION REQUIRED?   YES / NO

CAMPING PERMIT REQUIRED?   YES / NO

CELL RECEPTION: 📶   HIKING BUDDIES:

FACILITIES:
____

____

____

____

____

OVERALL RATING:

PHOTO / DRAWING:

NOTES & OBSERVATIONS:

MEMORABLE MOMENT:

HIKING LOG #24

HIKE/TRAIL NAME: ____

DATE: ________________   TYPE: → ONE WAY   ↻ LOOP   ⇄ OUT & BACK   ⛺ OVERNIGHT

START TIME: __________   LOCATION: ___________________________
                         (OR GPS)

END TIME: __________   LOCATION: ___________________________
                        (OR GPS)

DISTANCE: __________   ELEVATION: __________ ⇧ __________ ⇩

WEATHER: ☀   ⛅   ☁   🌧   ⛈   ❄   🌡 ________

TRAIL CONDITION: WILD   ◯ ◯ ◯ ◯ ◯   WELL USED

TRAIL TRAFFIC: LIGHT   ◯ ◯ ◯ ◯ ◯   HEAVY

DIFFICULTY LEVEL: EASY   ◯ ◯ ◯ ◯ ◯   HARD

FUN FACTOR: DULL   ◯ ◯ ◯ ◯ ◯   AMAZING

TRAIL RESERVATION REQUIRED?   YES / NO

CAMPING PERMIT REQUIRED?   YES / NO

CELL RECEPTION: ▁▂▃▅   HIKING BUDDIES:

                                      ____

FACILITIES: ___________________________

                                      ____

(P)   🚹🚺   🐾   ___________________________

🚰   ⛱   ⛺   ___________________________

                                      ____

OVERALL RATING: 

PHOTO / DRAWING:

NOTES & OBSERVATIONS:

MEMORABLE MOMENT:

HIKING LOG #25

HIKE/TRAIL NAME: ____

DATE: _______________   TYPE: ONE WAY   LOOP   OUT & BACK   OVERNIGHT

START TIME: _______   LOCATION: _______________________________
                        (OR GPS)

END TIME: _______   LOCATION: _______________________________
                      (OR GPS)

DISTANCE: _______   ELEVATION: _______ ⇧   _______ ⇩

WEATHER:

TRAIL CONDITION: WILD ◯ ◯ ◯ ◯ ◯ WELL USED

TRAIL TRAFFIC: LIGHT ◯ ◯ ◯ ◯ ◯ HEAVY

DIFFICULTY LEVEL: EASY ◯ ◯ ◯ ◯ ◯ HARD

FUN FACTOR: DULL ◯ ◯ ◯ ◯ ◯ AMAZING

TRAIL RESERVATION REQUIRED?   YES / NO

CAMPING PERMIT REQUIRED?   YES / NO

CELL RECEPTION: HIKING BUDDIES:

FACILITIES: _______________________________

                         ____

                         ____

                         ____

                         ____

OVERALL RATING:

PHOTO / DRAWING:

NOTES & OBSERVATIONS:

MEMORABLE MOMENT:

HIKING LOG #26

HIKE/TRAIL NAME: ____

DATE: _________________ TYPE: → ONE WAY   ↻ LOOP   ⇄ OUT & BACK   OVERNIGHT

START TIME: ____________ LOCATION: _________________________________
                          (OR GPS)

END TIME: _____________   LOCATION: _________________________________
                          (OR GPS)

DISTANCE: ____________   ELEVATION: __________ ⇧   __________ ⇩

WEATHER: ☀ ⛅ ☁ 🌧 ⛈ ❄ 🌡 ______

TRAIL CONDITION: WILD   ○ ○ ○ ○ ○   WELL USED

TRAIL TRAFFIC: LIGHT ○ ○ ○ ○ ○   HEAVY

DIFFICULTY LEVEL: EASY   ○ ○ ○ ○ ○   HARD

FUN FACTOR: DULL   ○ ○ ○ ○ ○   AMAZING

TRAIL RESERVATION REQUIRED?   YES / NO

CAMPING PERMIT REQUIRED?   YES / NO

CELL RECEPTION: HIKING BUDDIES:
                            ____
FACILITIES: _______________________________
                            ____
                            ____
                            ____

OVERALL RATING:
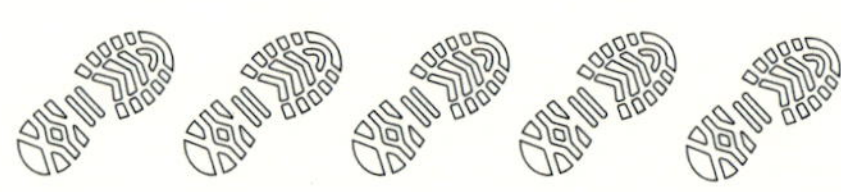

PHOTO / DRAWING:

NOTES & OBSERVATIONS:

MEMORABLE MOMENT:

HIKING LOG #27

HIKE/TRAIL NAME: ____

DATE: _________________ TYPE: ONE WAY LOOP OUT & BACK OVERNIGHT

START TIME: __________ LOCATION: _______________________________
(OR GPS)

END TIME: __________ LOCATION: _______________________________
(OR GPS)

DISTANCE: __________ ELEVATION: __________ ⇧ __________ ⇩

WEATHER: ☀ ⛅ ☁ 🌧 ⛈ ❄ 🌡 _______

TRAIL CONDITION: WILD ○ ○ ○ ○ ○ WELL USED

TRAIL TRAFFIC: LIGHT ○ ○ ○ ○ ○ HEAVY

DIFFICULTY LEVEL: EASY ○ ○ ○ ○ ○ HARD

FUN FACTOR: DULL ○ ○ ○ ○ ○ AMAZING

TRAIL RESERVATION REQUIRED?   YES / NO

CAMPING PERMIT REQUIRED?   YES / NO

CELL RECEPTION: HIKING BUDDIES:

FACILITIES:
____

____

____

____

____

OVERALL RATING:

PHOTO / DRAWING:

NOTES & OBSERVATIONS:

MEMORABLE MOMENT:

HIKING LOG #28

HIKE/TRAIL NAME: _______________________

DATE: _______________ TYPE: → ONE WAY   ↻ LOOP   ⇄ OUT & BACK   OVERNIGHT

START TIME: _________ LOCATION: _______________
                       (OR GPS)

END TIME: _________ LOCATION: _______________
                     (OR GPS)

DISTANCE: _________ ELEVATION: _______ ⇧ _______ ⇩

WEATHER: ☀ ⛅ ☁ 🌧 ⛈ ❄ 🌡 _______

TRAIL CONDITION: WILD ○ ○ ○ ○ ○ WELL USED

TRAIL TRAFFIC: LIGHT ○ ○ ○ ○ ○ HEAVY

DIFFICULTY LEVEL: EASY ○ ○ ○ ○ ○ HARD

FUN FACTOR: DULL ○ ○ ○ ○ ○ AMAZING

TRAIL RESERVATION REQUIRED? YES / NO

CAMPING PERMIT REQUIRED? YES / NO

CELL RECEPTION: 📶   HIKING BUDDIES:

FACILITIES:
____

____

____

____

____

OVERALL RATING:

PHOTO / DRAWING:

NOTES & OBSERVATIONS:

MEMORABLE MOMENT:

HIKING LOG #29

HIKE/TRAIL NAME: _______________________

DATE: _______________ TYPE: ONE WAY   LOOP   OUT & BACK   OVERNIGHT

START TIME: _______ LOCATION: _______________
(OR GPS)

END TIME: _______ LOCATION: _______________
(OR GPS)

DISTANCE: _______ ELEVATION: _______ ⇑ _______ ⇩

WEATHER:

TRAIL CONDITION: WILD ◯ ◯ ◯ ◯ ◯ WELL USED

TRAIL TRAFFIC: LIGHT ◯ ◯ ◯ ◯ ◯ HEAVY

DIFFICULTY LEVEL: EASY ◯ ◯ ◯ ◯ ◯ HARD

FUN FACTOR: DULL ◯ ◯ ◯ ◯ ◯ AMAZING

TRAIL RESERVATION REQUIRED? YES / NO

CAMPING PERMIT REQUIRED? YES / NO

CELL RECEPTION: HIKING BUDDIES:

____

____

FACILITIES:

____

____

OVERALL RATING:

PHOTO / DRAWING:

NOTES & OBSERVATIONS:

MEMORABLE MOMENT:

HIKING LOG #30

HIKE/TRAIL NAME: _______________________

DATE: _______________ TYPE: ONE WAY   LOOP   OUT & BACK   OVERNIGHT

START TIME: __________ LOCATION: _______________________
(OR GPS)

END TIME: __________ LOCATION: _______________________
(OR GPS)

DISTANCE: __________ ELEVATION: __________ ⬆ __________ ⬇

WEATHER:

TRAIL CONDITION: WILD ◯ ◯ ◯ ◯ ◯ WELL USED

TRAIL TRAFFIC: LIGHT ◯ ◯ ◯ ◯ ◯ HEAVY

DIFFICULTY LEVEL: EASY ◯ ◯ ◯ ◯ ◯ HARD

FUN FACTOR: DULL ◯ ◯ ◯ ◯ ◯ AMAZING

TRAIL RESERVATION REQUIRED?   YES / NO

CAMPING PERMIT REQUIRED?   YES / NO

CELL RECEPTION: HIKING BUDDIES:
____
____
FACILITIES:
____
____
____
____

OVERALL RATING:

NOTES & OBSERVATIONS:

MEMORABLE MOMENT:

HIKING LOG #31

HIKE/TRAIL NAME: _______________________________

DATE: _______________   TYPE:

ONE WAY   LOOP   OUT & BACK   OVERNIGHT

START TIME: _______   LOCATION: _______________
(OR GPS)

END TIME: _______   LOCATION: _______________
(OR GPS)

DISTANCE: _______   ELEVATION: _______ ⇧   _______ ⇩

WEATHER:

TRAIL CONDITION: WILD ◯ ◯ ◯ ◯ ◯ WELL USED

TRAIL TRAFFIC: LIGHT ◯ ◯ ◯ ◯ ◯ HEAVY

DIFFICULTY LEVEL: EASY ◯ ◯ ◯ ◯ ◯ HARD

FUN FACTOR: DULL ◯ ◯ ◯ ◯ ◯ AMAZING

TRAIL RESERVATION REQUIRED?   YES / NO

CAMPING PERMIT REQUIRED?   YES / NO

CELL RECEPTION: HIKING BUDDIES:

____

FACILITIES: _______________________

____

____

____

____

OVERALL RATING:

PHOTO / DRAWING:

NOTES & OBSERVATIONS:

MEMORABLE MOMENT:

HIKING LOG #32

HIKE/TRAIL NAME: _________________________________

DATE: _________________ TYPE: → ONE WAY   ↻ LOOP   ⇄ OUT & BACK   OVERNIGHT

START TIME: _________ LOCATION: _________________________
(OR GPS)

END TIME: _________ LOCATION: _________________________
(OR GPS)

DISTANCE: _________ ELEVATION: _________ ⇧   _________ ⇩

WEATHER: ☀ ⛅ ☁ 🌧 ⛈ ❄ 🌡

TRAIL CONDITION: WILD ◯ ◯ ◯ ◯ ◯ WELL USED

TRAIL TRAFFIC: LIGHT ◯ ◯ ◯ ◯ ◯ HEAVY

DIFFICULTY LEVEL: EASY ◯ ◯ ◯ ◯ ◯ HARD

FUN FACTOR: DULL ◯ ◯ ◯ ◯ ◯ AMAZING

TRAIL RESERVATION REQUIRED?   YES / NO

CAMPING PERMIT REQUIRED?   YES / NO

CELL RECEPTION: ▂▃▅█   HIKING BUDDIES:

____

FACILITIES:

____

____

____

____

OVERALL RATING: 

PHOTO / DRAWING:

NOTES & OBSERVATIONS:

MEMORABLE MOMENT:

HIKING LOG #33

HIKE/TRAIL NAME: _______________________________

DATE: ______________ TYPE: → ONE WAY ↻ LOOP ⇄ OUT & BACK ⛺ OVERNIGHT

START TIME: __________ LOCATION: _______________________
(OR GPS)

END TIME: __________ LOCATION: _______________________
(OR GPS)

DISTANCE: __________ ELEVATION: __________ ⇧ __________ ⇩

WEATHER: ☀ ⛅ ☁ 🌧 ⛈ ❄ 🌡

TRAIL CONDITION: WILD   ◯ ◯ ◯ ◯ ◯   WELL USED

TRAIL TRAFFIC: LIGHT   ◯ ◯ ◯ ◯ ◯   HEAVY

DIFFICULTY LEVEL: EASY   ◯ ◯ ◯ ◯ ◯   HARD

FUN FACTOR: DULL   ◯ ◯ ◯ ◯ ◯   AMAZING

TRAIL RESERVATION REQUIRED?   YES / NO

CAMPING PERMIT REQUIRED?   YES / NO

CELL RECEPTION: 📶   HIKING BUDDIES:
____

FACILITIES:
____

____

____

OVERALL RATING:

NOTES & OBSERVATIONS:

MEMORABLE MOMENT:

HIKING LOG #34

HIKE/TRAIL NAME: _______________________________

DATE: _______________   TYPE: ONE WAY   LOOP   OUT & BACK   OVERNIGHT

START TIME: _______________   LOCATION: _______________
(OR GPS)

END TIME: _______________   LOCATION: _______________
(OR GPS)

DISTANCE: _______________   ELEVATION: _______________ ⇑   _______________ ⇓

WEATHER:

TRAIL CONDITION: WILD   ◯ ◯ ◯ ◯ ◯   WELL USED

TRAIL TRAFFIC: LIGHT   ◯ ◯ ◯ ◯ ◯   HEAVY

DIFFICULTY LEVEL: EASY   ◯ ◯ ◯ ◯ ◯   HARD

FUN FACTOR: DULL   ◯ ◯ ◯ ◯ ◯   AMAZING

TRAIL RESERVATION REQUIRED?   YES / NO

CAMPING PERMIT REQUIRED?   YES / NO

CELL RECEPTION: HIKING BUDDIES:
____
____

FACILITIES:
____
____
____
____

OVERALL RATING:

PHOTO / DRAWING:

NOTES & OBSERVATIONS:

MEMORABLE MOMENT:

HIKING LOG #35

HIKE/TRAIL NAME: _______________________

DATE: _______________ TYPE: → ONE WAY ↻ LOOP ⇄ OUT & BACK ⌂ OVERNIGHT

START TIME: _______________ LOCATION: _______________
(OR GPS)

END TIME: _______________ LOCATION: _______________
(OR GPS)

DISTANCE: _______________ ELEVATION: _______________ ⇧ _______________ ⇩

WEATHER:

TRAIL CONDITION: WILD ○ ○ ○ ○ ○ WELL USED

TRAIL TRAFFIC: LIGHT ○ ○ ○ ○ ○ HEAVY

DIFFICULTY LEVEL: EASY ○ ○ ○ ○ ○ HARD

FUN FACTOR: DULL ○ ○ ○ ○ ○ AMAZING

TRAIL RESERVATION REQUIRED?   YES / NO

CAMPING PERMIT REQUIRED?   YES / NO

CELL RECEPTION: HIKING BUDDIES:
____

FACILITIES:
____

____

____

____

OVERALL RATING:

PHOTO / DRAWING:

NOTES & OBSERVATIONS:

MEMORABLE MOMENT:

HIKING LOG #36

HIKE/TRAIL NAME: _______________________________________

DATE: _________________   TYPE: → ○ ⇄ ⛺
                                    ONE WAY   LOOP   OUT & BACK   OVERNIGHT

START TIME: _________   LOCATION: _______________________
                          (OR GPS)

END TIME: _________   LOCATION: _______________________
                        (OR GPS)

DISTANCE: _________   ELEVATION: _________ ⇧ _________ ⇩

WEATHER: ☀ ⛅ ☁ 🌧 ⛈ ❄ 🌡 _______

TRAIL CONDITION: WILD   ○ ○ ○ ○ ○   WELL USED

TRAIL TRAFFIC: LIGHT   ○ ○ ○ ○ ○   HEAVY

DIFFICULTY LEVEL: EASY   ○ ○ ○ ○ ○   HARD

FUN FACTOR: DULL   ○ ○ ○ ○ ○   AMAZING

TRAIL RESERVATION REQUIRED?   YES / NO

CAMPING PERMIT REQUIRED?   YES / NO

CELL RECEPTION: 📶   HIKING BUDDIES:
                                        ____
FACILITIES: _______________________
                                        ____
                                        ____
                                        ____
                                        ____

OVERALL RATING:

PHOTO / DRAWING:

NOTES & OBSERVATIONS:

MEMORABLE MOMENT:

HIKING LOG #37

HIKE/TRAIL NAME: _______________________________

DATE: _________________   TYPE: ONE WAY   LOOP   OUT & BACK   OVERNIGHT

START TIME: _____________   LOCATION: _______________________
(OR GPS)

END TIME: _____________   LOCATION: _______________________
(OR GPS)

DISTANCE: _____________   ELEVATION: __________ ⬆   __________ ⬇

WEATHER:

TRAIL CONDITION: WILD   ◯ ◯ ◯ ◯ ◯   WELL USED

TRAIL TRAFFIC: LIGHT   ◯ ◯ ◯ ◯ ◯   HEAVY

DIFFICULTY LEVEL: EASY   ◯ ◯ ◯ ◯ ◯   HARD

FUN FACTOR: DULL   ◯ ◯ ◯ ◯ ◯   AMAZING

TRAIL RESERVATION REQUIRED?   YES / NO

CAMPING PERMIT REQUIRED?   YES / NO

CELL RECEPTION: HIKING BUDDIES:
____
____
FACILITIES:
____
____
____
____

OVERALL RATING:

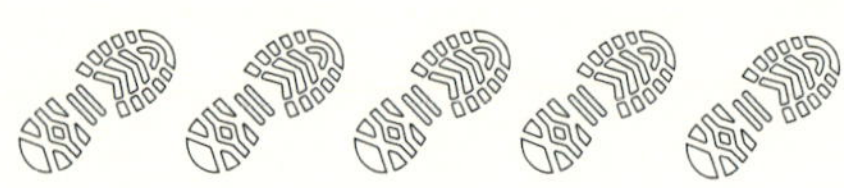

PHOTO / DRAWING:

NOTES & OBSERVATIONS:

MEMORABLE MOMENT:

HIKING LOG #38

HIKE/TRAIL NAME: ____

DATE: _______________   TYPE: → ONE WAY   ↻ LOOP   ⇄ OUT & BACK   OVERNIGHT

START TIME: _______________   LOCATION: _______________________
(OR GPS)

END TIME: _______________   LOCATION: _______________________
(OR GPS)

DISTANCE: _______________   ELEVATION: _______________ ⇧ _______________ ⇩

WEATHER:

TRAIL CONDITION: WILD   ◯ ◯ ◯ ◯ ◯   WELL USED

TRAIL TRAFFIC: LIGHT   ◯ ◯ ◯ ◯ ◯   HEAVY

DIFFICULTY LEVEL: EASY   ◯ ◯ ◯ ◯ ◯   HARD

FUN FACTOR: DULL   ◯ ◯ ◯ ◯ ◯   AMAZING

TRAIL RESERVATION REQUIRED?   YES / NO

CAMPING PERMIT REQUIRED?   YES / NO

CELL RECEPTION:

HIKING BUDDIES:
____
____
____
____
____

FACILITIES:

OVERALL RATING:

PHOTO / DRAWING:

NOTES & OBSERVATIONS:

MEMORABLE MOMENT:

HIKING LOG #39

HIKE/TRAIL NAME: _______________________________

DATE: _______________   TYPE: → ONE WAY   ↻ LOOP   ⇄ OUT & BACK   ⛺ OVERNIGHT

START TIME: _______   LOCATION: _______________________
(OR GPS)

END TIME: _______   LOCATION: _______________________
(OR GPS)

DISTANCE: _______   ELEVATION: _______ ⇧   _______ ⇩

WEATHER: ☀   ⛅   ☁   🌧   ⛈   ❄   🌡 _______

TRAIL CONDITION: WILD ○ ○ ○ ○ ○ WELL USED

TRAIL TRAFFIC: LIGHT ○ ○ ○ ○ ○ HEAVY

DIFFICULTY LEVEL: EASY ○ ○ ○ ○ ○ HARD

FUN FACTOR: DULL ○ ○ ○ ○ ○ AMAZING

TRAIL RESERVATION REQUIRED?   YES / NO

CAMPING PERMIT REQUIRED?   YES / NO

CELL RECEPTION: 📶   HIKING BUDDIES:

____

FACILITIES:

____

____

____

OVERALL RATING:

PHOTO / DRAWING:

NOTES & OBSERVATIONS:

MEMORABLE MOMENT:

HIKING LOG #40

HIKE/TRAIL NAME: _______________________________

DATE: _______________ TYPE: → ONE WAY   ↻ LOOP   ⇄ OUT & BACK   ⌂ OVERNIGHT

START TIME: _______________ LOCATION: _______________
(OR GPS)

END TIME: _______________ LOCATION: _______________
(OR GPS)

DISTANCE: _______________ ELEVATION: _______________ ⇧ _______________ ⇩

WEATHER:

TRAIL CONDITION: WILD ◯ ◯ ◯ ◯ ◯ WELL USED

TRAIL TRAFFIC: LIGHT ◯ ◯ ◯ ◯ ◯ HEAVY

DIFFICULTY LEVEL: EASY ◯ ◯ ◯ ◯ ◯ HARD

FUN FACTOR: DULL ◯ ◯ ◯ ◯ ◯ AMAZING

TRAIL RESERVATION REQUIRED?   YES / NO

CAMPING PERMIT REQUIRED?   YES / NO

CELL RECEPTION: HIKING BUDDIES:
                         ____
FACILITIES: _______________________
                         ____
                         ____
                         ____
                         ____

OVERALL RATING:

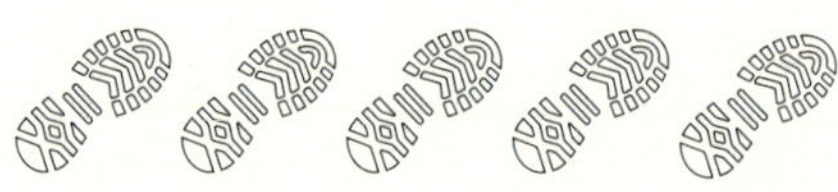

PHOTO / DRAWING:

NOTES & OBSERVATIONS:

MEMORABLE MOMENT:

HIKING LOG #41

HIKE/TRAIL NAME: _______________________

DATE: _______________ TYPE: → ONE WAY   ↻ LOOP   ⇄ OUT & BACK   ⛺ OVERNIGHT

START TIME: _______ LOCATION: _______________
(OR GPS)

END TIME: _______ LOCATION: _______________
(OR GPS)

DISTANCE: _______ ELEVATION: _______ ⇧ _______ ⇩

WEATHER: ☀ ⛅ ☁ 🌧 ⛈ ❄ 🌡 _______

TRAIL CONDITION: WILD ○ ○ ○ ○ ○ WELL USED

TRAIL TRAFFIC: LIGHT ○ ○ ○ ○ ○ HEAVY

DIFFICULTY LEVEL: EASY ○ ○ ○ ○ ○ HARD

FUN FACTOR: DULL ○ ○ ○ ○ ○ AMAZING

TRAIL RESERVATION REQUIRED? YES / NO

CAMPING PERMIT REQUIRED? YES / NO

CELL RECEPTION:

FACILITIES:

HIKING BUDDIES:
____
____
____
____
____
____

OVERALL RATING:

PHOTO / DRAWING:

NOTES & OBSERVATIONS:

MEMORABLE MOMENT:

HIKING LOG #42

HIKE/TRAIL NAME: _______________________________

DATE: _______________   TYPE: → ONE WAY   ↻ LOOP   ⇄ OUT & BACK   ⌂ OVERNIGHT

START TIME: __________   LOCATION: ____________________
(OR GPS)

END TIME: __________   LOCATION: ____________________
(OR GPS)

DISTANCE: __________   ELEVATION: __________ ⇧   __________ ⇩

WEATHER:

TRAIL CONDITION: WILD   ◯ ◯ ◯ ◯ ◯   WELL USED

TRAIL TRAFFIC: LIGHT   ◯ ◯ ◯ ◯ ◯   HEAVY

DIFFICULTY LEVEL: EASY   ◯ ◯ ◯ ◯ ◯   HARD

FUN FACTOR: DULL   ◯ ◯ ◯ ◯ ◯   AMAZING

TRAIL RESERVATION REQUIRED?   YES / NO

CAMPING PERMIT REQUIRED?   YES / NO

CELL RECEPTION: HIKING BUDDIES:

____

FACILITIES:

____

____

____

____

OVERALL RATING:

PHOTO / DRAWING:

NOTES & OBSERVATIONS:

MEMORABLE MOMENT:

HIKING LOG #43

HIKE/TRAIL NAME: _______________________________

DATE: _______________ TYPE: ONE WAY   LOOP   OUT & BACK   OVERNIGHT

START TIME: _______________ LOCATION: _______________
(OR GPS)

END TIME: _______________ LOCATION: _______________
(OR GPS)

DISTANCE: _______________ ELEVATION: _______________ ⇧ _______________ ⇩

WEATHER:

TRAIL CONDITION: WILD ◯ ◯ ◯ ◯ ◯ WELL USED

TRAIL TRAFFIC: LIGHT ◯ ◯ ◯ ◯ ◯ HEAVY

DIFFICULTY LEVEL: EASY ◯ ◯ ◯ ◯ ◯ HARD

FUN FACTOR: DULL ◯ ◯ ◯ ◯ ◯ AMAZING

TRAIL RESERVATION REQUIRED? YES / NO

CAMPING PERMIT REQUIRED? YES / NO

CELL RECEPTION: HIKING BUDDIES:

FACILITIES:
____
____
____
____
____
____

OVERALL RATING:

PHOTO / DRAWING:

NOTES & OBSERVATIONS:

MEMORABLE MOMENT:

HIKING LOG #44

HIKE/TRAIL NAME: _______________________

DATE: _______________ TYPE: ONE WAY LOOP OUT & BACK OVERNIGHT

START TIME: _______ LOCATION: _______________
(OR GPS)

END TIME: _______ LOCATION: _______________
(OR GPS)

DISTANCE: _______ ELEVATION: _______ ⇑ _______ ⇓

WEATHER:

TRAIL CONDITION: WILD ○ ○ ○ ○ ○ WELL USED

TRAIL TRAFFIC: LIGHT ○ ○ ○ ○ ○ HEAVY

DIFFICULTY LEVEL: EASY ○ ○ ○ ○ ○ HARD

FUN FACTOR: DULL ○ ○ ○ ○ ○ AMAZING

TRAIL RESERVATION REQUIRED? YES / NO

CAMPING PERMIT REQUIRED? YES / NO

CELL RECEPTION: HIKING BUDDIES:
____
____
FACILITIES: _______________
____
____
____

OVERALL RATING:

PHOTO / DRAWING:

NOTES & OBSERVATIONS:

MEMORABLE MOMENT:

HIKING LOG #45

HIKE/TRAIL NAME: _______________________________

DATE: _______________ TYPE:

START TIME: _______________ LOCATION: _______________
(OR GPS)

END TIME: _______________ LOCATION: _______________
(OR GPS)

DISTANCE: _______________ ELEVATION: _______________ ⇧ _______________ ⇩

WEATHER:

TRAIL CONDITION:	WILD	○ ○ ○ ○ ○	WELL USED
TRAIL TRAFFIC:	LIGHT	○ ○ ○ ○ ○	HEAVY
DIFFICULTY LEVEL:	EASY	○ ○ ○ ○ ○	HARD
FUN FACTOR:	DULL	○ ○ ○ ○ ○	AMAZING

TRAIL RESERVATION REQUIRED? YES / NO

CAMPING PERMIT REQUIRED? YES / NO

CELL RECEPTION: HIKING BUDDIES:

____

FACILITIES:

____

____

____

____

OVERALL RATING: 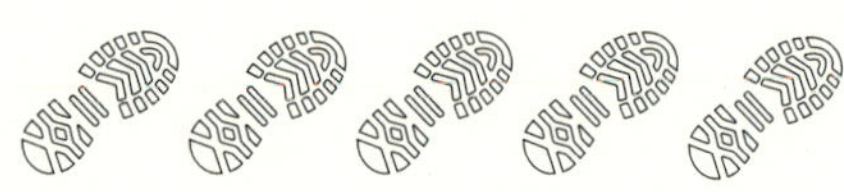

PHOTO / DRAWING:

NOTES & OBSERVATIONS:

MEMORABLE MOMENT:

HIKING LOG #46

HIKE/TRAIL NAME: _______________________

DATE: _______________   TYPE: → ONE WAY   ↻ LOOP   ⇄ OUT & BACK   OVERNIGHT

START TIME: _______   LOCATION: _______________
                        (OR GPS)

END TIME: _______   LOCATION: _______________
                      (OR GPS)

DISTANCE: _______   ELEVATION: _______ ⇧   _______ ⇩

WEATHER:

TRAIL CONDITION: WILD   ◯ ◯ ◯ ◯ ◯   WELL USED

TRAIL TRAFFIC: LIGHT   ◯ ◯ ◯ ◯ ◯   HEAVY

DIFFICULTY LEVEL: EASY   ◯ ◯ ◯ ◯ ◯   HARD

FUN FACTOR: DULL   ◯ ◯ ◯ ◯ ◯   AMAZING

TRAIL RESERVATION REQUIRED?   YES / NO

CAMPING PERMIT REQUIRED?   YES / NO

CELL RECEPTION: HIKING BUDDIES:

FACILITIES: _______________
                     ____
                     ____
                     ____
                     ____

OVERALL RATING:

PHOTO / DRAWING:

NOTES & OBSERVATIONS:

MEMORABLE MOMENT:

HIKING LOG #47

HIKE/TRAIL NAME: _________________________

DATE: _______________   TYPE: ONE WAY   LOOP   OUT & BACK   OVERNIGHT

START TIME: __________   LOCATION: _________________________
                             (OR GPS)

END TIME: __________   LOCATION: _________________________
                             (OR GPS)

DISTANCE: __________   ELEVATION: __________ ⇧   __________ ⇩

WEATHER:

TRAIL CONDITION: WILD   ◯ ◯ ◯ ◯ ◯   WELL USED

TRAIL TRAFFIC: LIGHT   ◯ ◯ ◯ ◯ ◯   HEAVY

DIFFICULTY LEVEL: EASY   ◯ ◯ ◯ ◯ ◯   HARD

FUN FACTOR: DULL   ◯ ◯ ◯ ◯ ◯   AMAZING

TRAIL RESERVATION REQUIRED?   YES / NO

CAMPING PERMIT REQUIRED?   YES / NO

CELL RECEPTION: HIKING BUDDIES:
                                 ____
FACILITIES: _________________________
                                 ____
                                 ____
                                 ____

OVERALL RATING:

PHOTO / DRAWING:

NOTES & OBSERVATIONS:

MEMORABLE MOMENT:

HIKING LOG #48

HIKE/TRAIL NAME: ___________________________

DATE: _______________ TYPE: → ONE WAY   ↻ LOOP   ⇄ OUT & BACK   ⛺ OVERNIGHT

START TIME: _______________ LOCATION: _______________
(OR GPS)

END TIME: _______________ LOCATION: _______________
(OR GPS)

DISTANCE: _______________ ELEVATION: _______ ⇧   _______ ⇩

WEATHER: ☀ 🌤 ☁ 🌧 ⛈ ❄ 🌡___

TRAIL CONDITION: WILD ◯ ◯ ◯ ◯ ◯ WELL USED

TRAIL TRAFFIC: LIGHT ◯ ◯ ◯ ◯ ◯ HEAVY

DIFFICULTY LEVEL: EASY ◯ ◯ ◯ ◯ ◯ HARD

FUN FACTOR: DULL ◯ ◯ ◯ ◯ ◯ AMAZING

TRAIL RESERVATION REQUIRED?   YES / NO

CAMPING PERMIT REQUIRED?   YES / NO

CELL RECEPTION: ▁▂▃▄   HIKING BUDDIES:

____

____

____

FACILITIES:

🅟 👤👤 🐾

🚰 🪑 ⛺

____

____

OVERALL RATING:

PHOTO / DRAWING:

NOTES & OBSERVATIONS:

MEMORABLE MOMENT:

HIKING LOG #49

HIKE/TRAIL NAME: _______________________________

DATE: _______________ TYPE: → ONE WAY   ↻ LOOP   ⇄ OUT & BACK   ⛺ OVERNIGHT

START TIME: _______________ LOCATION: _______________________
(OR GPS)

END TIME: _______________ LOCATION: _______________________
(OR GPS)

DISTANCE: _______________ ELEVATION: _________ ⇧ _________ ⇩

WEATHER:

TRAIL CONDITION: WILD ◯ ◯ ◯ ◯ ◯ WELL USED

TRAIL TRAFFIC: LIGHT ◯ ◯ ◯ ◯ ◯ HEAVY

DIFFICULTY LEVEL: EASY ◯ ◯ ◯ ◯ ◯ HARD

FUN FACTOR: DULL ◯ ◯ ◯ ◯ ◯ AMAZING

TRAIL RESERVATION REQUIRED?   YES / NO

CAMPING PERMIT REQUIRED?   YES / NO

CELL RECEPTION: HIKING BUDDIES:
____
____
____

FACILITIES:
____
____
____

OVERALL RATING:

PHOTO / DRAWING:

NOTES & OBSERVATIONS:

MEMORABLE MOMENT:

HIKING LOG #50

HIKE/TRAIL NAME: ___________________________

DATE: _______________   TYPE:

ONE WAY   LOOP   OUT & BACK   OVERNIGHT

START TIME: _______________   LOCATION: _______________
(OR GPS)

END TIME: _______________   LOCATION: _______________
(OR GPS)

DISTANCE: _______________   ELEVATION: _______________ ⇧   _______________ ⇩

WEATHER:

TRAIL CONDITION: WILD ◯ ◯ ◯ ◯ ◯ WELL USED

TRAIL TRAFFIC: LIGHT ◯ ◯ ◯ ◯ ◯ HEAVY

DIFFICULTY LEVEL: EASY ◯ ◯ ◯ ◯ ◯ HARD

FUN FACTOR: DULL ◯ ◯ ◯ ◯ ◯ AMAZING

TRAIL RESERVATION REQUIRED?   YES / NO

CAMPING PERMIT REQUIRED?   YES / NO

CELL RECEPTION: HIKING BUDDIES:

FACILITIES:
____

____

____

____

____

OVERALL RATING: 

PHOTO / DRAWING:

NOTES & OBSERVATIONS:

MEMORABLE MOMENT:

HIKING LOG #51

HIKE/TRAIL NAME: _________________________________

DATE: ________________   TYPE: → ONE WAY   ↻ LOOP   ⇄ OUT & BACK   ⛺ OVERNIGHT

START TIME: __________   LOCATION: _________________________
                         (OR GPS)

END TIME: __________   LOCATION: _________________________
                        (OR GPS)

DISTANCE: __________   ELEVATION: __________ ⇧   __________ ⇩

WEATHER: ☀   ⛅   ☁   🌧   ⛈   ❄   🌡 _______

TRAIL CONDITION:	WILD	◯ ◯ ◯ ◯ ◯	WELL USED
TRAIL TRAFFIC:	LIGHT	◯ ◯ ◯ ◯ ◯	HEAVY
DIFFICULTY LEVEL:	EASY	◯ ◯ ◯ ◯ ◯	HARD
FUN FACTOR:	DULL	◯ ◯ ◯ ◯ ◯	AMAZING

TRAIL RESERVATION REQUIRED?   YES / NO

CAMPING PERMIT REQUIRED?   YES / NO

CELL RECEPTION: HIKING BUDDIES:

FACILITIES: _________________________________

____

____

____

____

OVERALL RATING:

PHOTO / DRAWING:

NOTES & OBSERVATIONS:

MEMORABLE MOMENT:

HIKING LOG #52

HIKE/TRAIL NAME: ____________________

DATE: ____________ TYPE: ONE WAY   LOOP   OUT & BACK   OVERNIGHT

START TIME: ____________ LOCATION: ____________
(OR GPS)

END TIME: ____________ LOCATION: ____________
(OR GPS)

DISTANCE: ____________ ELEVATION: ____________ ⇧ ____________ ⇩

WEATHER:

TRAIL CONDITION: WILD ◯ ◯ ◯ ◯ ◯ WELL USED

TRAIL TRAFFIC: LIGHT ◯ ◯ ◯ ◯ ◯ HEAVY

DIFFICULTY LEVEL: EASY ◯ ◯ ◯ ◯ ◯ HARD

FUN FACTOR: DULL ◯ ◯ ◯ ◯ ◯ AMAZING

TRAIL RESERVATION REQUIRED? YES / NO

CAMPING PERMIT REQUIRED? YES / NO

CELL RECEPTION: HIKING BUDDIES:

____

____

____

FACILITIES:

____

____

OVERALL RATING:

PHOTO / DRAWING:

NOTES & OBSERVATIONS:

MEMORABLE MOMENT:

Hiking Tips

Our top 10 tips for a successful day out in the wilderness

1. GET THE RIGHT BOOTS AND SOCKS

Blisters and sore feet can ruin an otherwise awesome hike, so be sure to invest in quality hiking shoes and socks. Visit your local outdoor shop and get fitted for boots that match your unique fit – snug but not tight. Don't skimp on socks either. Wool or synthetic socks are the way to go - avoid cotton. Also, remember to carry blister dressings just in case.

2. CHECK THE CONDITIONS

Always check the weather forecast before setting out. Use local forecasts rather than national as they're more accurate. Weather apps can be useful too. With this information you can select the right clothing for the day. Poor weather often contributes to accidents and can make the whole experience disappointing, so if you're just starting out then pick a fine day with little chance of rain.

3. DRESS FOR SUCCESS

It's important to wear the right clothing, and layers are the key. Avoid cotton as it'll just absorb sweat and make you cold. Wool and synthetics are recommended. You'll need a waterproof jacket, a thermal layer (e.g. fleece) and ideally a wicking base layer to keep you dry and warm. A hat is also a must – a cap for the summer, or a beanie for the colder weather. Polarized sunglasses will help protect your eyes from the sun and give you clearer vision.

4. PROTECT YOURSELF

You need to think about what you'll need throughout your hike, and what could make the difference if you do get lost, or something bad happens. Carrying a few dry matches and a flashlight could save your life if you get into a search and rescue situation. We've compiled an "Essential Gear List" on the opposite page with our suggestions to ensure you have everything you need for a safe and enjoyable hike.

5. TAKE FOOD AND WATER

Water is probably the most important thing you can bring on a hike. Consider if water will be available along the route. Taking too much water will weigh you down, but not enough can be dangerous. It's recommended to drink 1 litre of water for every 2 hours of hiking, but that will be temperature dependent. For a day-hike, its best to bring high energy food that doesn't need refrigeration or heating. Common choices include energy bars, trail mix, dried fruit and jerky. You don't need to over-do it, just make sure you've got enough to fuel you on your journey. Then throw in another granola bar for good measure.

6. KEEP IT LIGHT

So, despite telling you to pack all this gear, it's also important to pack light. You want to try and find the lightest and smallest of each item. For example, don't carry a 12oz sunscreen around – a travel pack will be plenty.

7. TELL SOMEONE WHERE YOU'RE HEADING

It's so simple and yet easy to overlook. Tell someone where and when you'll be hiking – if something bad does happen your chances of being found are dramatically improved. Designate a "check-in" window of time that allows for delays like minor detours, admiring amazing views or a sprained ankle. That way your friend won't worry if you're a bit late.

8. PACE YOURSELF

It's all about the enjoying the journey. There's no need to race through the hike to get to that stunning view – it'll still be there whenever you arrive. You need to find a pace you're comfortable with and can sustain all day. It might feel weird at first, but after a few miles, especially uphill, you'll be glad you saved your energy. Stop for breaks when you need them and enjoy the hiking experience.

9. FIND SOME TRAIL BUDDIES

For beginners, it's advisable to start off with a partner or group. It's enjoyable to share the experience as well as being safer, plus, it's someone you can split the planning and preparations with! Bring a friend (or friends) along. Once you get some experience under your belt, you can begin to explore solo hiking.

10. LEAVE NO TRACE

It's important to take care of the beautiful trails we love so they stay beautiful. Take time to read about the seven principles of the Leave No Trace ethos and be sure to follow them. It's the responsibility of everyone to take care of our natural spaces.

ESSENTIAL	GEAR		LIST
CELL PHONE	TRAIL MAP	COMPASS	SUNSCREEN
FIRST AID KIT	FOIL BLANKET	WHISTLE	DRY MATCHES
HEADLAMP	FOOD	WATER	SUNGLASSES
POCKET KNIFE	BLISTER DRESSINGS	EXTRA CLOTHES	HAT

HIKING LINGO

Terminology you'll hear out on the trail

BASE WEIGHT: The weight of the gear you're carrying, not including food, water, fuel, and the clothes on your back.

BEAVER FEVER: Slang term for Giardiasis - a parasitic infection of the digestive system most commonly contracted from unfiltered water. Symptoms include bloating and diarrhea.

BLAZE: A colored marker, usually painted or nailed to a tree, to help guide you along the trail. Color-coded systems help to determine which trail you're on. (Also see Trail Marker)

BUSHWHACKING: Hiking off the trail. Sometimes because you are lost, and sometimes just for the adventure of it.

CACHE: A location on or near a trail where you store water, food and gear before a long hike, in order to resupply without leaving the trail.

CAMEL UP: A technique of drinking a lot of water at a water source to avoid having to carry as much water on the hike.

CATHOLE: A 6" hole dug in the ground to dispose of your poop. Ideally located 200 ft from trails, campsites, and water sources.

COL: The lowest point on the ridge between two peaks where you stop descending one peak and start ascending the next one. Also called a "notch" or a "saddle".

CONTOUR LINE: A line drawn on a topographic map that shows the elevation. The distance between the lines reveals the gradient.

COWBOY CAMP: To camp out under the stars (instead of in a tent or shelter)

GAITERS: Protective clothing that bridges the gap between your boots and pants, preventing mud, stones & snow getting in. Get waterproof ones to keep your pants dry!

HANGER: Hunger induced anger - when you're hangry, your decision making is impaired and negative emotions increase.

HIKER BOX: A box where hikers may take or leave items such as food and gear free of charge - often found along long distance-trails at hostels and gear stores.

HIKER TAN: The layer of dust and dirt on a hiker's skin (especially their legs) that makes them appear tanned until they wash it off.

HYOH: "Hike Your Own Hike" – the idea that you should hike a trail how you want to, and not worry about what others are doing.

PURIST: Someone who hikes every step of a trail without deviating or setting foot on side trails.

REGISTER: A book kept at hostels, trail angel houses etc. that hikers can sign and leave messages for other hikers behind them.

SAND-BAGGING: To intentionally or unintentionally describe a route as easier than it is.

SAR: "Search and Rescue" – an organization that helps people who are injured or lost whilst hiking in the backcountry, many of which are entirely volunteer-led..

SCRAMBLING: Using your hands and feet to climb up rocks and boulders

SUCKER HOLE: A short spate of good weather that gives you false hope that the bad weather has passed.

SWITCHBACKS: Sharp zigzag turns in a trail that allow you to ascend a slope at a less severe angle than travelling straight uphill.

THRU-HIKE: Hiking the entirety of a long-distance trail from end to end, typically in one season.

TRAIL ANGEL: A person who helps hikers out with rides, food, or trail magic (see below)

TRAIL MAGIC: A random act of kindness or item found on the trail – anything from a cooler full of sodas sitting at a trail crossing, to transportation into town or overnight accommodation.

TRAIL MARKER: Purposefully created marks along trails to show hikers they are on the right path. These vary by region and can include cairns, blazes, flagging, small tags, or signs. They are often brightly colored to stand out from the landscape and are usually attached to trees. In areas without trees, stakes driven into the ground topped by a marker or paint may be used.

TRAIL MIX: A common snack eaten on hikes, which varies by region and personal preference but generally contains a mix of granola, seeds, nuts and dried fruit.

TRIPLE CROWNER: Someone who has hiked all three "big" long-distance trails in the US: the Appalachian Trail (AT), the Pacific Crest Trail (PCT), and the Continental Divide Trail (CDT).

VEGGIE BELAY: To grab onto vegetation and use it as a rope when descending or ascending steep slopes.

HIKING BUCKET LIST

The all-time greatest places & trails you'd love to hike

COMPLETE

Visit our website to check out our other
titles and get exclusive discounts!

www.dorsland-press.com

Made in United States
North Haven, CT
11 December 2022